The author's thanks to the National Cotton Council of America and to the many experts and workers in the textile field whose valuable suggestions based on knowledge and experience helped in the writing of this book.

SIXTH PRINTING

Library of Congress Catalog Card Number: 53-8607
Printed in the United States of America by Polygraphic Co. of America

The FIRST BOOK of COTTON

BY
Matilda Rogers

PICTURES BY
Mimi Korach

FRANKLIN WATTS, INC.
575 LEXINGTON AVENUE
NEW YORK 22, N. Y.

Cotton for you

Cotton growing in the fields is a beautiful sight. Its young leaves shoot upward through the earth to form a green pattern across the plantations. Its flowers star the plants with delicate color. As the season lengthens, the seed pods spill out their fluffs to turn the cotton acres snowy white. But cotton is useful, too. For thousands of years it has been harvested all over the world to be made into cloth. Its history is long and exciting.

Today, this white fluff that bursts out on cotton bushes in midsummer is used for many, many things. Possibly you are wearing cotton—a cotton shirt and slacks or dungarees, or a cotton dress. The curtains at the windows in the living room and the slipcovers on the chairs may be made of cotton. Almost all household "linen," which long ago was really made of linen, is made of cotton nowadays.

You think of these things almost at once. But there are many more uses of cotton. There's the "paper" money in Dad's wallet. It contains a small amount of cotton. The tires on the family car may contain cotton. In making the cake she baked for lunch, Mother may have used a cooking oil—and the chances are it was made from cottonseed. Other vegetable oils are used for cooking, too, but cottonseed oil is one of the leading ones. Margarine is made of it, too.

On board ship, heavy sheets of cotton canvas are used to cut off wind and rain from parts of decks, to cover deck cargoes, and to protect lifeboats when not in use.

Fishermen's high rubber boots are often reinforced with cotton on the inside. Yachts and some fishing boats have cotton sails. Cotton fuzz, called "linters," is used in making artificial leather, rayon and furniture stuffing.

And there are the all-important sporting goods! The lining of your catcher's mitt is made of cotton. There's some in a baseball. The tops of the sneakers you wear are made of it. The heavy net of the basket into which basketball players toss the ball to make a goal—that, too, is made of cotton.

The paper you write on in school and the pages of the books you study and read for fun contain fibers from cotton rags. And of course there is cotton cloth in the bindings of books.

Engineers who run the engines of trains and ships and those who run machinery in factories all use cotton rags to wipe away extra oil and keep the machinery clean. Millions of pounds of rags and waste cotton threads are sold each year just for this.

Hospitals couldn't get along without cotton. Sheets, pillowcases and towels, some of the uniforms and caps that nurses wear, and doctors' white jackets are made of cotton. Most important is the sterile absorbent cotton used in such great quantities to dress wounds, to disinfect and to clean, as well as the sterile gauze and adhesive tape used in making bandages.

Even the electricity that lights our lamps and runs our radios and vacuum cleaners comes into our homes through wires incased in rubber and cotton.

Dairy cattle are fed on crushed cottonseed hulls and cottonseed meal, and produce good rich milk for us. Beef cattle supplied with cottonseed feed give us good meat.

And look at our portable radios. The cabinets are made of plastic, which is sometimes manufactured from cottonseed hulls.

All this is only a small cross section of the cotton in our lives. Cotton's uses are so many that all of them could not possibly be listed here.

Cotton is such an important crop that the part of our Southern states where it can be grown is known as the "Cotton Belt." The work of getting cotton ready for all of us to use has become an important part of industry the country over. Railroads help the cotton industry, too. They carry raw cotton to factories. Millions of dollars change hands in the buying and selling of the many products made from cotton lint and seeds. In one way or another, millions of workers find employment in connection with cotton—in field and factory, as it is shipped by freight steamers and railroad, and when it is sold in shops. No wonder that cotton is sometimes called "King Cotton"!

A fiber with a story

Raw cotton is a natural fiber—a threadlike and slightly curly fluff or "lock" attached to cotton seeds in much the same way that milkweed's fluff is fastened to its seeds. Nature has grown these fluffs on some seeds so that winds can blow them far away from the plant on which they grew and spread them over a wide area. For if all the seeds fell straight down under the plants and tried to take root there, they would crowd each other badly and too many would be choked and would die. A number of plants have such fluff attached to their seeds. A dandelion is one that almost everyone knows.

Cotton fiber is naturally very convenient for use in making cloth. It is from one inch to one inch and three-quarters long—quite long, as plant fibers grow. And it is strong, yet soft and easily bent, too. Best of all is the natural curl or slight twist in it. Any fibers that are to be made into yarn for weaving have to be twisted so that they will hold together. Raw cotton is already partly prepared for man's use.

11

It is not surprising then that cotton was one of the earliest fibers used by mankind. Cotton cloth has been found in ruins thousands of years old. Ancient legends of the Far East spoke of cotton fluffs as "vegetable lambs."

The people of India were the first to spin and weave cotton fabric. Traders took small quantities of it into other nearby lands. From there, other traders carried it farther. It reached China, Persia, Babylonia and Egypt. It changed hands so often among the traders that the people of these lands who finally bought it for their own use could not find out where it had come from originally. It was expensive, so that only the wealthy could afford it. An emperor or a prince was proud to have a garment of fine cotton.

12

It was several centuries before some of these people learned that this wonderful fabric had first come from India. Even then, they themselves did not start cultivating the cotton plant immediately. Cotton-planting did spread gradually, however, many centuries before the birth of Christ. Seeds were bought from traders, and cotton began to be grown in many places.

In India and China, climate and soil combined to produce cotton with a short fiber, called "short-staple" cotton. But in Egypt a kind with a longer fiber developed. The excellence of this cotton became known in time to the people of the growing countries of Europe.

When America began to be settled by Europeans it was discovered that the fine warm climate of the Southern colonies was suitable for cotton-growing. About ten years after Jamestown was settled in 1607 cotton seeds from Egypt, brought on long voyages in sailing ships, were sold to Virginians. And so the first North American colonial crop of cotton was planted. England urged the settlers to grow more and more of it as time went on, for she could make use of all she could get. From Virginia, cotton-growing spread to other regions of the South.

To make the crop pay the planters well, large fields of cotton had to be grown. The big landowners looked around for cheap labor. Slave-traders then saw their chance to make money as never before. More and more Negroes were captured in their villages in Africa, shipped to America, and sold to the growers. Their work produced tons of cotton and made the South rich.

Much of the raw cotton was shipped to England, where spinners and weavers, working in their homes, were kept busy making cotton cloth. This became a thriving industry. England sold cotton cloth to many other countries.

14

In America at that time most women made their own yarn and cloth on spinning wheels and hand looms. But there was always a demand in America for English goods, too. Those well-to-do families who could afford them bought the English goods for clothes and household uses. Men needed sailcloth for their ships, also.

By the middle of the 1700s, English cloth was beginning to be made in mills instead of in the workers' homes. Later, after the colonies had won their independence from England, the young United States keenly felt the need for cotton spinning and weaving mills of its own. Several attempts were made at starting the industry in America, but the people of the new country were poorly equipped for it. Finally, in 1790, Samuel Slater, not long after arriving from England, established a mill in Pawtucket, Rhode Island, which became a success. It was the beginning of an industry in which New England grew to be a leader. About the time the Civil War was fought and the slaves were freed, more machines were being invented, and the uses of cotton grew.

Today the United States is the leading cotton-producing country of the world. It produces about 40 per cent of the world's cotton. The many other cotton-growing lands, all together, produce the other 60 per cent.

Cotton is grown in some surprising places. Some of the cotton-growing lands we all know. Others we seldom think of as cotton-producers. India, China, Egypt, the Soviet Union and Brazil are the leading growers after the United States. Turkey, Mexico and Peru are a few of the many others.

India is still the largest cotton-grower next to the United States, but hers is very short-staple cotton and of a rather poor grade. Egypt, on the other hand, does not have a very large crop because the country is rather small and the farm-land areas are mostly narrow strips along the great River Nile. But her farmers make up in quality what they do not have in quantity. They produce especially good long-staple cotton, which is much needed in making certain fine fabrics. Almost every modern textile country buys some cotton from Egypt.

As with all American field crops, our scientists are always improving cotton. They have crossbred different varieties and grown them in various ways. By this means they have developed several kinds of short-, medium- and long-staple cotton. Some varieties grow particularly well in regions that have good rainfall. Others grow well in arid regions where the land must be irrigated. Most cotton grows best in the warmest regions, though some varieties may grow well at the northern edge of the Cotton Belt where the .climate is cooler and the growing season shorter.

The green areas show where cotton is grown in the United States

In modern textile industry, cotton of different staple-lengths is used for making different fabrics. Manufacturers buy only the particular kind they need for the products they make.

Once upon a time, farmers planted all kinds of cotton without thinking about the length of the fiber. Manufacturers bought it and mixed all the cotton from many farms together. Nowadays, farmers plant their fields with only one kind of cotton that they know is wanted. When a manufacturer buys from a farm he knows that all the cotton from that particular plantation has exactly the same kind of short or long staple.

17

Cotton long ago

The ancient Egyptians knew of cotton. Centuries and centuries before the birth of Christ they raised this fiber for weaving into cloth.

As early as 502 B. C., the Chinese knew of cotton. However, they used silk and were not interested in cotton as cloth until much later. At first, they grew it as a decorative garden flower.

18

The great Italian artist Leonardo da Vinci was so interested in cotton and its spinning that in 1519 he invented a U-shaped device to fit around a spinning machine's spindle and improve its working.

Aztec records of long ago show that these people of Mexico were skilled cotton workers years before Cortes' invasion in 1519. This ancient piece of picture writing shows a cotton weaver.

Long before the Spaniards invaded Peru in 1531 the Peruvian people used cotton. These are some of their spinning and weaving tools. The old Peruvian vase shows a woman spinning cotton.

19

Cotton around the world

Men load cotton onto river boats along the Nile in Egypt. It will be taken to the seaport of Alexandria, and from there will be sent to various other countries.

In the African Sudan, cotton often goes to market by camelback.

Brazil is becoming an important cotton-growing country. Here new land is being cleared for this important crop.

In far-off China, this cotton is being carried to market in huge wheelbarrows.

In parts of India, many cotton fields are still plowed by oxen.

Raising the cotton crop

To grow well, the cotton plant needs a warm climate, much sunshine, rich soil, and, of course, water. It has to have a long growing season—about six and one-half months between the last frost of spring and the first cold days of autumn.

The states of the Southeastern seaboard and of the Gulf regions have enough rainfall for the crop. But in other areas of our Cotton Belt, especially in the San Joaquin Valley of California and in New Mexico and Arizona, water has to be channeled into the fields to irrigate them.

Planting starts early in the spring. In southern Texas it is often warm enough around the first of March for the farmers to plant. Farther north, the farmers wait until April.

22

First they must prepare the fields. The plowing, once done with horse-drawn plows, is now carried out largely by using those wonderful work-saving machines, tractors. But in rolling hill country horse-drawn plows are still used, and also, of course, on many of the smaller farms. Some farmers plow with one horse, others use bigger plows, drawn by two, three or even four horses or mules. These plows make many furrows at once.

Tractor plows work best on large, level fields, and by far the largest part of the cotton-growing land is flat. The tractors are not only used for plowing, but have thirty different attachments that can be put on for all kinds of other work.

23

After a field has been plowed, the farmer attaches the "planter bedder" to his tractor. This prepares the furrows and plants the seeds.

A *planter-bedder machine*

Some of these planters make two furrows, others make four or more. The furrows to be planted are spaced from three to five feet apart to give the plants plenty of room as they grow. The cotton seeds, which are held in bucket-like containers, slide out of openings and fall into the soil. The man driving the machine can regulate the planting so that the seeds are just the right distance apart and so that not too many fall in the same place. Recent tests have shown that the bushes bear more cotton if they are placed only about six inches apart in each row.

As soon as the seeds are in the ground, the machine covers them lightly with earth and presses it down firmly.

Leaving plenty of space between the rows is important, for then the spreading branches can develop well and later on it is possible for the hot sunshine to fall on all the ripening cotton fiber. Sunlight is needed to produce cotton of good quality. All this the farmer thinks of as he drops the seeds.

About ten days after the planting, tiny green shoots push out of the seeds and up through the earth. Soon after that, when the plants are about three inches high, the farmer hires workers to do the weeding. Weeding means taking out not only the many weeds that spring up, but also thinning out extra plants wherever several sprouts come up too close together. The farm workers who do this are called "hoe hands" or "cotton-choppers." Today, more and more of this weeding and chopping is done by machines.

The cotton plants grow steadily and soon become bushes that grow from three feet to six feet high, depending on the kind of cotton, the region where it grows, the climate, soil, and the amount of water the plant gets.

Weeding by machine

26

About six weeks after planting, buds appear on the cotton branches. At first, these are very small, but they become large and plump under the hot sun. In another three weeks they open and the large cotton flowers unfold their petals. Usually they are light in color—white or cream-white —and become light lavender or pink on about the third day. In shape and size they look somewhat like small hollyhock blossoms.

In a few days the fragile petals of the first flowers fall off, leaving tiny green pods—the beginning of the important cotton fiber. These soon grow into firm green "bolls," which a little later become the size of a walnut. As other buds develop, the plant has buds, blossoms and seed pods at the same time.

Boll weevil
(greatly enlarged)

Larva
(greatly enlarged)

The all-important cotton fiber starts early to form inside the bolls. Then the farmer's real worries begin, for many things can go wrong with his cotton from this time on.

Insects and diseases may harm his crop. Chief trouble-maker for many years has been the boll weevil. This insect is grayish-brown and about the size of a small housefly. Boll weevils originally came to the United States from Mexico. They have destroyed millions of dollars' worth of cotton in the years since their arrival.

With their pointed snouts the females puncture the hard shells of flower buds or bolls and lay their eggs inside them. In a short while the eggs hatch and the young insects, called "larvae," begin to eat the contents of the buds or bolls.

28

To prevent as much boll weevil damage as possible, the farmer dusts the plants with a chemical that kills the insects. He does this in the evening between five and nine when the boll weevils are most active. The farmer must handle the dusting chemical carefully, for it is poisonous to man and animals. However, it does not injure the plants.

He drives through the field with a fixed-nozzle "cotton-duster" which can reach many rows of cotton plants at one time. Or he may use an airplane which flies very low. Many growers with very large fields do cotton-dusting in this way, or hire someone to do it for them.

If it rains within twenty-four hours after the dusting, the farmer may have to do his work again. Within this time the weevils may not yet have died and as rain washes away the poison they revive and go right on destroying cotton. Because the cotton plants need moisture to grow, however, the rain is most welcome at other times.

Dusting a cotton field

The round green bolls grow steadily larger and more plump. In six to nine weeks they are about the size of hens' eggs. Meanwhile the farmer keeps busy with other work. For one thing, he will want to strip the leaves from his cotton plants. When leaves are thick on the bushes at cotton-picking time, the work is slowed up for the pickers. If they do not work slowly and carefully they will get many leaves into their bags with the cotton. Some chemicals have been developed in recent years that do a remarkably good job of "defoliation," or taking off the leaves. These chemicals are sprayed on the plants in somewhat the same way that the dusting chemicals for insects are applied. The chemicals wither the leaves without harming the bolls in any way. The farmer has to be sure he uses only the best of such products, and those that have been well tested. Otherwise he might harm the bolls and lower the value of his cotton.

All the while, the cotton bolls have been growing steadily and the fiber inside them has grown longer. It has curved back on itself over and over again to pack itself into the closed pod. The seeds to which it is attached grow riper and darker while the green boll that holds them begins to turn brown.

In time the boll becomes so tightly packed with ripe fiber that it is ready to burst open. The heat of the sun helps by drying out the boll on its now leafless branch, so that it finally splits along natural seams into hard, dry sections, of which there are sometimes four, sometimes five. These turn outward and slightly downward, exposing the white fiber. After three or four more days of sunshine the bolls are completely opened. As the fiber dries and becomes fluffy, it overflows its burst boll.

The fields turn so white with their fluffs that they look as though they were covered with snow. The time has come to pick the cotton. If this is not done quickly, rain may come and damage the crop by beating fiber out of the bolls onto the muddy ground. Or strong winds may blow the ripe cotton through the air. That harms it, too. The farmers anxiously watch the sky, hoping rain will stay away until the crop is safely gathered in. Long before this time they have made arrangements for the cotton-picking. And now the pickers arrive.

31

Harvesting the crop

Many farmers hire a number of people to pick their cotton. They may hire five or six or thirty or forty, depending on how large their fields are. Other farmers have the work done by mechanical pickers.

Mechanical pickers—some types are called "strippers"—are a fairly new invention. They have been used only in the past ten or twelve years, and there are already several different kinds. They are really tractors with the picker machinery attached.

A picker works in this way: At the front of the tractor engine are fastened several metal shafts that are half open. They are shaped somewhat like upended troughs. On the inner side are rows of metal fingers which interlace. They begin to turn as the tractor starts moving down the rows. The sides of the trough take hold of the now leafless cotton bushes and press them toward the picking fingers. These pluck the soft fiber fluffs, which are loose in the dry bolls and give way easily. The fingers are close together, and though the cotton fiber can pass between them, most of the stems and dry bolls stay outside and drop to the ground. Then the fingers turn and pull the cotton inside to another shaft.

The cotton, once it is in the inner shaft, is combed, or plucked, off the fingers by another part of the machine. Then blower pipes float it up into the "basket," as it is called. The walls of this big compartment are sometimes made of fine metal mesh, so that the snowy heap can be seen growing larger and larger as the machine works its way down the rows. The compartment usually holds about 750 pounds of cotton. When it is full it is emptied into a big truck.

A mechanical picker can gather much more cotton than a man working only with his two hands. A person picks from two hundred to three hundred, and sometimes even four hundred pounds a day, working very long hours. A mechanical picker harvests from eight thousand to thirty thousand pounds in the same time. It does the work of forty or more people.

Mechanical pickers are still very expensive and are used mostly by owners of very large plantations. However, in some areas, owners of small farms can rent them. Many of them do.

To make the mechanical pickers more widely usable, plant breeders are developing short-branched rather than long-branched cotton plants. Mechanical pickers can pluck cotton more easily from these short-branched plants.

Mechanical cotton pickers

Most of the cotton in the United States is still picked by hand, however. Workers, hand-picking, get fewer dry stems and pieces of bolls in with their cotton than machines do. Such dirt in cotton may stain the fiber. Too, it makes the cleaning process more difficult later on at the mills. Waste in cotton lowers its value in the eyes of buyers, also. Mechanical pickers are constantly being improved, however, and should do a cleaner picking job in time.

The farmer hires the cotton-picking workers through an agency in a nearby town. In California and some other regions, companies especially organized to handle the picking make contracts with the farmers and take over this work. They do all the hiring of pickers, they oversee the work as it goes on, and they pay the pickers' wages. The farmer in turn pays the contractor.

The cotton-pickers—men, women and children—come into the fields early in the morning, just after sunrise. The straps of the long canvas cotton sacks which they call "pick sacks" are placed around their waists or over their shoulders. This leaves both their hands free for picking the cotton fluffs. As most of the pickers are used to the work, their fingers move nimbly over the bushes.

Early in the morning, when the air is still cool, and the workers feel fresh from the night's sleep, they can work quickly. But as the sun rises higher and higher the heat grows intense. The cotton-growing regions are in temperate or sub-tropical zones and have very hot midsummers. The temperature is often at 112 degrees in many Southern fields. The workers have to slow down in order to be able to endure the heat.

Cotton-picking is monotonous, but the pickers have each other for company and sometimes they find ways of breaking the dullness. Negro workers, with their love of music and their fine voices, often sing together as they pick. Some of their beautiful melodies which have been handed down from one generation to another have been collected and are well known.

Whenever a cotton-picker's bag is full he takes it to the end of the row and over to the weighing place. Here a record is made of how many pounds the full bag weighs, and the cotton is emptied into a truck. The picker then goes back into the fields and starts filling his bag again.

Cotton-picking goes on for many days in the big fields. The farmers hope that good weather will last. They listen to weather reports on the radio with more interest than usual, and are glad if there is a real "dry spell" so that no cotton will be harmed. Sometimes a thundershower comes. That's bad enough, but not as serious as several days of rainy weather. Cotton will dry out soon after a brief, light shower, but a good soaking, especially with strong winds blowing, can do very great harm. Usually, however, since the Cotton Belt has many days and nights of dry weather in midsummer and late summer, most of the cotton is gathered in safely.

By the time the cotton-pickers have stripped a field of its ripe cotton once, the later ripening bolls are open. Then the men, women and children go through the field again. This second crop is not quite as bountiful as the first, but still it is worth collecting.

When all the crop on a farm has been gathered, the pickers leave to seek work elsewhere. Now the fields look bare and brown. The farmer puts a set of cutting instruments on the tractor, cuts the stalks down to the ground, and carts them off. They will be sold to be made into fertilizer and plastics. He plows his acres and gets the field ready for the next crop. But the farmer does not replant cotton in this same field. Instead he gives the field a change by sowing corn or some other crop. In this way he does not overuse the soil minerals that cotton plants especially need. As some of the stalks of the new crop are plowed into the soil after the harvest, and as fertilizer is put in too, the field is enriched. When the farmer plants cotton there again, the following year, he will have good soil and can be sure of a good crop.

At the cotton gin

But what has happened to the cotton which the pickers gathered?

With many people working in the field, the first truck is soon full. As fast as trucks are loaded, new ones move up to take their places and the full ones start on their way to the "cotton gin." This is a machine that separates the cotton seeds from the fiber.

If the farm is a very large one, the owner may have a gin on his own plantation. But most growers take their cotton to a gin located in some central place convenient to all the farmers in that area. Often it is in the nearest town. The farmer bringing cotton there can attend to other business, also. He may meet a buyer and arrange to sell his cotton, or he may go to the bank or attend to an errand at the grocer's.

The truck is driven under an air shaft in the gin shed and air sucks the cotton upward into the gin. There it first goes through a process by which bits of dry stems and earth are

At the cotton gin

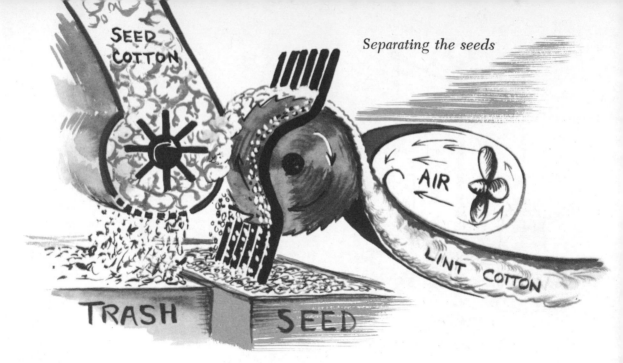

SEED COTTON

AIR

LINT COTTON

TRASH

SEED

blown and beaten out. Then the seeds are drawn out of the cotton by other machinery. The cotton fiber, or "lint," is pulled through a kind of grille made of bars set closely together. The openings between the bars are too small to let the seeds pass. Instead, the seeds drop into a large box that is carried on a conveyor to a storage place. Later, they are hauled off to factories where oil will be pressed out of them for various uses.

These seeds are the size of a small bean. There are only about eight in one cotton fluff, but they are much the heaviest part, weighing almost two-thirds of the whole boll. Once they were considered pure waste. Today they are a very valuable part of the cotton crop.

41

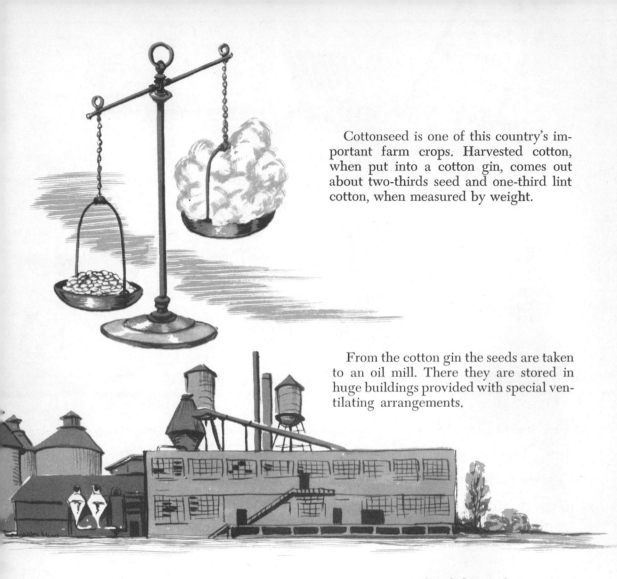

Cottonseed is one of this country's important farm crops. Harvested cotton, when put into a cotton gin, comes out about two-thirds seed and one-third lint cotton, when measured by weight.

From the cotton gin the seeds are taken to an oil mill. There they are stored in huge buildings provided with special ventilating arrangements.

On the outside of the seeds is a short fuzz called "linters." This is cut off by machinery and used to make plastics, artificial leather, varnishes and many other products.

The valuable cotton seeds

Next, the hulls of the seeds are taken off, to be used in making plastics or as feed for livestock.

After the linters and hulls are removed, the remaining kernels run through a machine which crushes the oil from them. Margarine and cooking and salad oils are made from cottonseed oil.

The meal that is left after oil has been crushed from the cottonseed makes valuable food for livestock.

A cotton bale

Now let's follow the ginned fiber, called lint. It is ready for baling as soon as the seeds have been taken out. Portions of it, each weighing about 480 pounds, are put into a machine and pressed tightly together until they become firm blocks about 54 inches long, 46 inches wide, and 27 inches high. Each of these is a "cotton bale," which is now covered with jute or burlap and bound with steel bands. The wrappings weigh about 20 pounds, so a bale ready for shipping weighs 500 pounds.

Sometimes the farmer sells his cotton right away, straight from the gin. But at other times he takes it back to his own barn to hold until he can get a better price for it. Or he may have his bales stored in a cotton warehouse near the gin. When this is done, his initials as well as a gin number are stamped on the burlap covering. At the warehouse, a government tag is attached to it. This stored cotton is like money in the bank for the farmer who owns it. Its value is so real he can borrow money on it from the bank. Of course, he sells the cotton as soon as he finds a good buyer for it. This usually does not take very long.

Once the bales are sold to a manufacturer, they are shipped to his mill by train, river boat or truck. Or, if the cotton is sold for export to some foreign land, it is shipped by ocean freighter. For long-distance shipping the cotton bale is compressed still further, so that it becomes one-half the size of the original bale. Space on ships is valuable and the less room the bale occupies, the better.

A cotton bale sometimes is bought and sold several times before it reaches a manufacturer and is made into thread and yarn and woven into cloth. Or again, a manufacturer may buy a whole cotton crop directly from the farmer. Sooner or later, however, the cotton bales arrive at the mills.

Loading bales on a freighter

At the yarn mill

There are many large yarn and cloth mills in the United States, and they have the finest, most modern power machines in the world. New England, which for over a century and a half was the leader of this industry, still has many mills. But now some of these mills spin and weave wool and other fibers besides cotton. The South now has 80 per cent of the cotton mills of this country. It was natural that this should happen, for time and the expense of shipping are saved if the mills are in the area where the fiber is grown.

Cotton has to go through many processes before it becomes dress material or sewing thread or whatever is to be made of it.

First the cotton bales go to a "yarn mill." At the yarn mill, workmen remove the bands and covering from the bales.

After the bales have been hand-stripped of bands and burlap, the cotton is passed into a machine with many steel spikes, which is called an "opener." Here the matted fibers are pulled apart. The loosened lint is

A cotton opener

mixed with the lint from many other cotton bales that have been dumped into this same room.

The manufacturer knows just what grades of cotton he is blending here and what fiber length they are. Tests were made of samples from the bales before he bought them.

The loosened, blended lint is next blown through large pipes into a machine called a "picker." There it is blown and beaten over a grille so that bits of boll and soil fall out. The very shortest fibers, which are really just fuzz, are blown out too, for they are not used in yarn-making. They are kept, however, and sold for other uses such as making plastics, furniture stuffing, and artificial leather.

All the rest of the cotton is then passed from the picker onto several big rollers which make a broad, flat layer of it,

47

A cotton picker

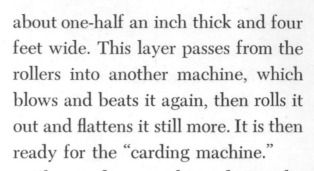
Coiling sliver into cans

about one-half an inch thick and four feet wide. This layer passes from the rollers into another machine, which blows and beats it again, then rolls it out and flattens it still more. It is then ready for the "carding machine."

The carding machine draws the layer out very wide and thin over quickly turning cylinders with wide spikes in them. And finally the layer is fed onto a narrower cylinder. This narrower layer, or "lap," of cotton now goes over another spiked roller which combs and cleans it still more and narrows it down to a loose, fuzzy rope one inch in diameter. This rope is called "sliver."

Several of these slivers are doubled one over the other and are then drawn through rollers once more. This doubling and rolling evens out the cotton fibers and draws them all in the same direction. The carded slivers come out of this machine about the same thickness as before but much improved in smoothness. For convenient handling they are coiled in cans about one yard high.

These cans of loose ropes of cotton are taken to machines which draw them out and smooth them again. And finally they are given a light twist. They come out as soft yarn very much thinner than the slivers—really just about the thickness of a lollipop stick. This is called "roving." Other machines thin the roving still more. As it leaves the last machine, the roving is wound on big spools called "bobbins," then stacked ready for spinning.

The spinning machines are huge and swift. A single spinning frame often has 200 to 250 "spindles," the twirling rods on which bobbins are placed. Some of the larger frames have over 300 spindles. They whirl away at terrific speed, unwinding the bobbins and twisting the loose yarns many times, drawing them out tightly to make them finer. They combine several of these fine threads next, twisting them together and drawing them out once more. So the threads or yarns, which were at first loose and weak, become firmer and stronger. Just how long they are spun and how hard or soft they finally are depends on how they are to be used.

Spinning yarn

To make knitting yarns, the strands are rather lightly twisted, then wound up in loose skeins or hanks. To make sewing thread, they are twisted many more times. Yarn for weaving is twisted more lightly in the spinning than thread for sewing, and more tightly than yarn for knitting.

Sewing thread is made very firm. The many different thicknesses are given numbers. When shoppers go into a store to buy sewing thread they choose it by the numbers. If they want a fine thread to sew the seams of a chambray or gingham dress on a sewing machine, they buy size 60. In sewing coarser materials like sheeting or denim, they use heavier thread. There are many numbers from which to select. If buyers want to sew on buttons they may use the strong, coarse size 30, or even a heavier thread. The smaller the number, the heavier the thread.

The greatest part of the yarn or thread spun in the yarn mill, however, is for weaving cloth. And various lots of it must be prepared differently to make different kinds of cloth.

Yarn used to weave chambray is soft. It is much less tightly twisted than yarn made for twill or for denim or sailcloth. Look at almost any cotton goods in your house and compare the threads in the weaves. You will see that each—handkerchief, towel, mattress ticking, window curtain—is made of a slightly different-looking yarn. Yarn mills make hundreds of kinds of yarns. Each fills the particular need for some manufactured article.

Yarn for weaving, as well as that which is finally rolled on spools and sold as sewing thread, is put through a hot starchy bath called "sizing." This lightly pastes the yarn's small fibers together, strengthening it and giving it a smoother finish.

After the sizing, the yarn for weaving is ready for the cloth manufacturer.

Inventions that helped

Until 1733, cloth was woven by slowly passing a shuttle in and out by hand across the warp threads of cotton. Then John Kay invented a "fly shuttle," which passed swiftly back and forth in only one groove and made weaving easier and quicker. It was the first of many inventions which changed cotton cloth-making into an enormous, worldwide business.

In 1764, James Hargreaves invented a "spinning jenny," a hand machine which could spin eight strands of thread at once, instead of one, as old-fashioned spinning wheels did.

About 1768, Richard Arkwright built a spinning machine which was driven by a horse and later by water power. He called it a "spinning frame."

the cotton industry

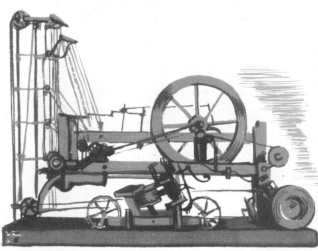

In 1779, Samuel Crompton improved upon Arkwright's and Hargreaves' machines by inventing his "mule," with spinning spindles on a movable carriage which stretched and twisted the cotton yarn. Crompton was too poor to patent his invention and sold it for a small sum. Years later, however, the English House of Commons granted him £5000.

Until 1793, seeds were picked from cotton by hand. Workers could clean only about one pound of cotton in a day. Then Eli Whitney, a young Northerner visiting on a Southern plantation, invented a hand machine called a "cotton gin," whose revolving spikes combed the seeds from fiber. It cleaned as much as fifty pounds in a day. Modern power cotton gins work in much the same way as Whitney's machine, but are larger and can gin more cotton daily.

53

Making cloth

Bobbins and beam

Down the highway leading from the yarn mill roar trucks on the way to the cloth mills. They are loaded with bobbins and with "beams," which are the removable parts of the weaving machines, or "looms." Around these beams the lengthwise threads for the cloth have been wound side by side and as close together as they will be in the finished cloth itself.

Some yarn mills supply themselves with beams which are just the right size to fit on the looms of the cloth mills which buy yarn from them. In this way they save those manufacturers the time and trouble of having to unwind the yarn and roll it on their own beams. Rewinding also has to be done if the yarn is delivered to the weavers on bobbins instead of on beams. Some manufacturers prefer it one way and some the other.

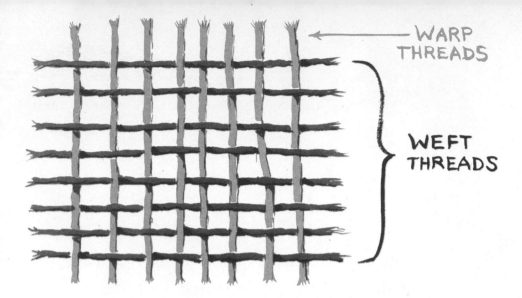

The loom beam has on it only the threads which will run lengthwise in the cloth. These lengthwise threads are called the "warp" threads. If you take a piece of cotton yard goods and begin counting the threads running lengthwise, you will realize how many thousands of warp threads there are on one beam. If the cloth is 40 inches wide and has 60 threads to an inch, the loom beam must have 2,400 separate threads on it!

On the power looms the ends of these thousands of threads from the beam are drawn through the "harness," which is built to guide the lengthwise threads in the process of weaving. When these warp threads are all in place, other yarn of the same kind but a shade finer and less strong is attached to the "shuttle" part of the machine. The shuttle carries thread back and forth across the lengthwise threads. This crosswise shuttle thread is the "woof" thread, sometimes also called "weft," or "filling."

When all the threads are ready, the worker who handles the loom touches a lever or button and sets the weaving machinery in motion.

At once the harness, to which the lengthwise or warp threads are attached, lifts up every other thread so that there is a space between these and the rest of the lengthwise threads. Through this space shoots the shuttle with the woof thread, or filling, attached. The harness then drops the first set of threads and raises the others. The woof thread passes through this new space on its way back. Now the weaver has started his piece of cloth. And it grows as the harness lifts first one set of lengthwise threads, then the other, and the woof thread shoots through.

Weaving cloth

On a modern power loom the warp and woof threads move at such terrific speed that the worker beside the loom sees the cloth forming by the foot, the yard, and the dozen yards in only a short while. If something goes wrong, the worker can stop the machine, correct the fault, and set the machine in motion again. Sometimes the machine stops itself. This happens when one of the threads breaks. The machine is idle until the workman has knotted the threads' broken ends together. Then it rushes on again.

As more and more of the material forms upon the loom, it goes along over a roller which carries it to an inspection table. This is equipped with a remarkable "electric eye"— a complicated device whose electric current is changed by the action of light. The cloth moves automatically across the table, where another worker stands and watches it. When the watcher sees a flaw that needs attention, he puts his hand between the light of the electric eye and the cloth. This breaks the beam of light and instantly stops the whole big machine. He marks the faulty spot, takes his hand away, and the machine goes on.

57

Inspecting cloth

Weaving a textured cloth

Plain weaving is a simple crossing of woof threads alternately over and under single warp threads. Fancier kinds of fabrics can be made by using several harnesses. These lift groups of two, three, or more threads, spaced in special ways. By varying the arrangements of the warp thread which the woof thread is to go over or under, a pattern is formed in the fabric. Many different patterns can be woven into the cloth, making such textures as twills. Specially built looms can weave very complicated patterns.

Fabric as it leaves the loom is from forty to one hundred yards in length, and is grayish-tan in color — the color of the raw lint. The only exception, of course, is when dyed yarns have been used in weaving. The grayish, freshly woven fabric is called "gray goods." Some of this freshly woven fabric is scoured, dried on rollers, and sold just as it is, as unbleached muslin. But more of it is taken away to be bleached and dyed. All this is done at the "finishing plant."

At the finishing plant

Various kinds of cotton cloth go through a number of processes here. First some are run swiftly between very hot plates that are set wide enough apart so that they barely touch the cloth. This singes off the fine outer fuzz of the yarns and gives the cloth a better surface. Then the material is scoured. Several tons of it at a time are put in big vats and soaked. Next they are bleached in a chlorine or peroxide bath, which whitens them.

Some of this bleached cloth becomes "white goods"— our sheets, materials for handkerchiefs, underwear and shirts.

Most cotton fabrics are preshrunk. This is done by a mechanical shrinking process such as is used in the production of fabrics labeled "Sanforized." When you see that word on a label inside a shirt or other garment, you know it will not shrink out of fit in washing, for the cloth was forced to do its shrinking at the finishing plant.

Other vast quantities of cloth are bleached to get them ready for dyeing or for printing.

Bleaching cloth

Often yarn is dyed before the cloth is woven

For many years, cotton fabrics were dyed in colors which faded easily. Now special dyes have been developed for cotton cloth — dyes known as "vat" dyes — which cannot be dissolved in water. Once the cloth has absorbed the dye, it is colorfast. Later, when the cloth is made into clothes, they will not fade in washing.

To dye cotton fabrics in solid colors, the bleached rolls of material from the looms are put on machines which run them through vats. The cloth comes out blue, pink, red, yellow or whatever other color the vat contained. As the fabrics are drawn out again by the movement of the machines, they are put through a rinse that removes any surplus dye. Next the fabrics go over hot rollers that dry, smooth and iron them, then roll them up again for convenient handling.

Printing undyed cotton cloth

If a design is to be printed on the cloth, the process is different. The white material is then run through sets of rollers, each of which has a part of the design engraved on it.

The cloth passes over a big central roller, around which the engraved rollers are set. Each touches the central roller at one point. Each is fed with the color it is to print. One may be black, another yellow, another pink, and so on, depending upon the particular design that is being printed. When the machine is set in motion and the cloth moves along over the big middle roller, the other rollers each print their part of the design at regular intervals. The cloth that glides out at the other side has the complete design on it.

Most materials, whether dyed or printed or white, are given a bath of caustic soda which makes them shiny and firm. This is called "mercerizing." And finally they are put through another bath containing a gentle, pastelike liquid that acts as a very light starch.

61

The last ironing of the cloth is done by a huge machine called a "calender," which presses the cloth under great force so that it comes out smooth and beautiful. Then it goes to machines which cut it into suitable lengths and either roll it tightly or arrange it in flat folds.

There are some new ways of treating cotton cloth which make it good for special uses. A checked, striped or plain cotton cloth can be treated with a recently developed chemical which makes it resist water. Pretty raincoats are made of this material.

By another process, fabrics are flameproofed. Curtains made of these cloths can be used in our homes as a safety measure against fires. But such fabrics are most often used in theaters or as circus tents, for in such places, where crowds gather, fire prevention is particularly important.

Cotton dress materials can be treated by a new method so that they do not crease easily. A dress made of such crease-resistant material looks neat and fresh longer than if made of cotton treated in the ordinary way.

Cotton cloth can be especially made to resist intense cold. Heavy cotton duck prepared in this way is made into sleeping bags. A person sleeping in one of these new duck bags can keep warm in a freezing temperature, as low as 40 degrees below zero. Yet the bag is light and easy to carry.

From the finishing plant, hundreds of thousands of rolls of many different kinds of fabrics are shipped to wholesalers and department stores. Countless other rolls go to manufacturers of every kind and are made into everything from overalls to evening dresses — even toy dogs and dolls. Finally, in stores everywhere, all of us buy things made of cotton, the fluffy fiber of a plant with a long, long history.

Cotton keeps

In factories large and small, machine workers manufacture cotton cloth into men's shirts and garments of many other kinds.

Testing cotton fiber and classing it by grade and length is work for other experts.

Laboratory chemists work on new sprays to destroy insect pests such as the boll weevil, or to help the cotton farmer in other ways.

64

many workers busy

Scientists continually seek ways of improving cotton cloth's quality. This man is making tests for dyes that will not fade in strong sunlight.

At some cloth mills, artists in large studios create colorful new designs for printing cotton fabrics.

Fashion designers continually produce new costumes made of cotton fabrics.

Do you know that--

Cotton wears longer than any other fabric in common use.

Cotton becomes stronger when wet.

Cotton absorbs moisture easily and dries quickly. This is one reason why it is good for swabs and bandages and for clothing in hot climates.

Cotton has a greater variety of uses than any other fiber. Scientists say there are now more than 10,000 uses for cotton.

One bale of cotton supplies enough material for 250 pairs of men's cotton trousers.

Each year about 10 million square yards of cotton cloth are used to make American flags.

In the past 21 years the boll weevil has eaten more cotton than all the people in the United States would use in six years.

When Columbus came to America in 1492, he found cotton growing in the West Indies.

The design of the early English textile machines was a closely guarded secret. No worker was allowed to make drawings of them or to tell how they operated. England hoped to keep the cotton industry to herself in this way. Samuel Slater first brought knowledge of these machines to America in 1789. For doing this, he would have been subject to arrest, if he had returned to England.

Cotton talk

Bale — 480 pounds of ginned cotton fiber, pressed into a block 54 inches long, 46 inches wide, and 27 inches high, covered with jute or burlap and bound with steel bands. Cotton is shipped to market in bales weighing about 500 pounds, with wrapping.

Beam — the removable part of a weaving loom, on which are wound lengthwise threads of the cloth which is to be woven.

Bobbin — a big spool on which cotton yarn is wound at the yarn mill.

Boll — the pod in which cotton seeds grow and which contains cotton fiber.

Boll weevil — an insect which destroys the cotton fiber by eating it in the boll.

Calender — a huge finishing machine which gives cotton cloth a final ironing after it has been bleached, dyed and mercerized.

Carding machine — a machine at the yarn mill which draws raw cotton fiber into a wide, thin layer and then into "sliver."

Cotton choppers — farm workers who hoe the cotton fields.

Cotton duster — a farm machine which kills boll weevils and other insects by spraying chemicals on the cotton plants.

Cotton gin — a machine which separates the raw cotton fiber from the seeds.

Defoliation — the chemical process of removing leaves from the plants by spraying before cotton-picking begins.

Fabric — a cloth made by weaving or knitting threads together.

Fiber — a thin, threadlike piece of material. Raw cotton is a fiber.

Finishing plant — the factory where cotton cloth is bleached and dyed.

Gin — to separate cotton fiber from seeds with a cotton gin.

Ginned cotton — raw cotton fiber from which the seeds have been removed at the cotton gin — also called "lint cotton."

Gray goods — freshly woven cotton cloth before it is bleached or dyed.

Harness — the part of a weaving loom that raises and lowers the lengthwise threads as the cloth is woven.

Lap — a narrow layer of raw cotton fiber, produced in the process of making cotton yarn.

Lint — the raw cotton fiber after it has been ginned and its seeds removed.

67

Linters — the short fibers which stick to cotton seeds after the long fibers have been ginned off.

Long-staple — long-length (used in speaking of cotton fiber).

Loom — a machine for weaving cloth.

Medium-staple — medium-length (used in speaking of cotton fiber).

Mercerizing — a process of treating cotton cloth with caustic soda to make it firm and shiny.

Opener — a machine that pulls apart the matted fibers of a cotton bale at the yarn mill.

Picker — a machine that cleans the cotton fiber after the bales are opened at the yarn mill.

Planter bedder — a machine attached to a tractor for use in planting cotton seeds.

Roving — a loose, thin rope of raw cotton fiber, produced in the process of making cotton yarn.

Sanforized — trademark denoting cotton preshrunk by a compressive machine, to prevent later shrinkage in washing.

Short-staple — short-length (used in speaking of cotton fiber).

Shuttle — the part of a weaving loom that carries the crosswise thread from one side of the cloth to the other.

Sizing — a starchy finish which strengthens and smooths cotton thread, yarn and cloth.

Sliver — a loose, fuzzy rope of raw cotton fiber about one inch in diameter, produced in the process of making cotton yarn.

Spindles — the upright, whirling rods of a spinning machine on which bobbins are placed and yarn spun.

Staple — the length and fineness of cotton fiber.

Stripper — a farm machine for harvesting cotton fiber.

Vat dyes — dyes which cannot be dissolved in water, so do not fade in washing.

Warp — the lengthwise threads of a piece of woven cloth.

Weft — the crosswise thread of a piece of woven cloth. Also called woof.

White goods — bleached, but undyed, cloth.

Woof — the crosswise thread of a piece of woven cloth.

Yarn mill — the mill at which cotton fiber is spun into thread for sewing and weaving.

Index